Advance Praise f

MW01025509

"Grace Schulman is a national treasure. This sumptuous array of splendid, hard-won poems feels in its essence like one poem, one surging grace note that sings out not only across years and oceans, but also across the great divide that separates the living from the dead and the knowable from the unknowable." —ROWAN RICARDO PHILLIPS

"*The Marble Bed* is magnificent. I am swept away by its trajectory and the luminescence of each poem. What a gift to the world this collection is."
—ELISE PASCHEN

"Grace Schulman's *The Marble Bed* confronts life and death matters. Here's a lyrical journey paced by sonnets that create a totalizing effect, with the surprise of jazz between tropes. This poet knows when, where, and what to leave out of lyrical portraits so the reader also helps to create meaning. We see and feel into the truth." —YUSEF KOMUNYAKAA

"In this profound, elegiac new volume, Grace Schulman seeks to immortalize as if in marble the sustaining power of love. . . . Schulman is our poet of, yes, grace, of elegance, and sorrow, of poems born out of the chiseled stone of reflection as they yearn and achieve transcendence."
—JILL BIALOSKY

"Grace Schulman's poems never forget we are all specks in the universe and sparkle only for a time. Her style is unruffled and her tone is controlled, but love and grief haunt the clarity of her mind."
—HENRI COLE

"Grace Schulman's newest collection is full of her lines of wonderment: she reveals both the rendered and unrendered world in all its difficult beauty. In her timely poems born of disjunctures—a 21st century pandemic, the early 17th century colonization of Montauk, New York, and in the voice of a caregiver or widow, traveler or gardener—she easily travels zones, cities, worlds: time. This is a much welcome and long-awaited book." —SOPHIE CABOT BLACK

BOOKS BY GRACE SCHULMAN

POETRY

The Marble Bed

Without a Claim

The Broken String

Days of Wonder: New and Selected Poems

The Paintings of Our Lives

For That Day Only

Hemispheres

Burn Down the Icons

MEMOIR

Strange Paradise: Portrait of a Marriage

TRANSLATION

Songs of Cifar: Poems (with Ann McCarthy de Zavala),
by Pablo Antonio Cuadra

At the Stone of Losses: Poems by T. Carmi

CRITICISM AND ESSAYS

Marianne Moore: The Poetry of Engagement

First Loves and Other Adventures

EDITIONS

The Poems of Marianne Moore (Authorized Edition)

Mourning Songs: Poems of Sorrow and Beauty

Ezra Pound: A Collection of Criticism

TURTLE POINT PRESS, *Brooklyn, New York*

GRACE SCHULMAN

The Marble Bed

Requests for permission to make copies of any
part of the work should be sent to:
Turtle Point Press, 208 Java Street, Fifth Floor, Brooklyn, NY 11222
info@turtlepointpress.com

Library of Congress Cataloging-in-Publication Data to come

Design by Alban Fischer Design

ISBN: 978-1-885983-83-1

Printed in the United States of America

First Edition

For Andy, Wendy, Emily, and David
and in memory of Jerome L. Schulman
(1927-2016)

Contents

Forgive me, distant wars, for bringing flowers home.

WISLAWA SZYMBORSKA

There are still songs to be sung
on the far side of humankind.

PAUL CELAN

Orchid

Not raised but found, this dancer, idling on trash,
abandoned in the compactor room,
fated to be smothered in a green bag,

its seven blooms startling, hot pink smiles
in deadpan weather, on the year's shortest
day, with the long night ahead. Gingerly,

sponging off ashes, eggshells, silvery
powder (talc, I hope), from its mossy planter,
I slide it toward high windows, and it changes

like fire: sherry to red-purple to magenta,
colors of blood, of beaujolais, of sin
and holiness, of saints on stained-glass panels,

light shining through, a diva's fan.
Fuchsia, the color named for a plant
that must have jolted Leonhart Fuchs,

the botanist, when he discovered it
in the 16th century, my orchid's
serious name is phalaenopsis,

for moths in flight. Its wingy blooms
blink, teasing, just out of eye's reach.
Sunsets they turn the color of red ochre

mixed with manganese, powdered and blown
through reeds by the early cave painters, fearful
of beasts, to glitter from a bison's frame;

I don't know the exact shade of red-purple
the Phoenicians used to dye robes for kings,
but I think this was it, also the color

of a rose Yeats set afire to see its ghost.
In my mind the ancient Egyptian
who painted amulets inside a royal tomb

wished only for this sizzling fuchsia
to wake the beloved dead, as he mixed gypsum
with rose madder in futile passion.

Once as a child I wandered in the park
bordering my usual asphalt streets,
and saw a flower, red-purple on a stem

with wings. I called to it, my angel.
Now I give an orchid air and water,
turn down the lumière, stroke the crooked stem

that darts out to reveal wings whose vermilion,
burning against a window facing brick,
defies endings on this cold year's end.

Happiness

is not a campfire
but an occulting light,
a field of fireflies
that blink on-off-on,

the tree you planted
whose apples
fall to the ground
half rotten, half sweet,

the street's jackhammers
that fall quiet at night,
the black skimmer's
white underside,

the life together,
apart, together,
the long marriage,
oxymoronic

in its dank joy.
Under a half-moon
quivering
through sycamores,

you held my body
half the night
as I lay in your arms,
sometimes half-awake,

speculating, well,
happy families are unalike.
I choose you
with your handicap,

your half-mobility,
not to mention
your leisure
in forsaking all others

for the chance
of our wholeness.
I take you,
my choice as certain

as plankton on sand
lights up
and arcs to the stars.

The Sand Dancers

In a faded photo, they dance on shore,
two kids we were, scuffing up bursts of sand;
hands rise and fall in a rapid step-slide-spin
on bumpy sand hills, seawater creeping closer.

They shimmy, high as gulls on one another
yet unaware they're skipping on a grave:
the black skull, once a horseshoe crab,
the jellyfish with blood-red intestines,

barnacles stuck fast on eyeless stones
nodding at them like beheaded saints,
seaweed like green hair rising in terror,
commemorate the shipwrecked off this coast,

voyagers and whalers, catch-fishermen.
Now the dancers join hands and swing out,
moonwalk on rocks sea-polished into eggs.
Fresh as sea foam, bright as the break and shuffle

of a long wave gone white before it roars,
its turbulence their only orchestra,
how could they know the years would bring
losses, wars, together, apart, together?

Now it's heel-toe, as if they didn't hear
the clink of a buoy warning of danger
as the chill wind lifts a wave's underbelly
to gather force and strike, all in its time.

Fragments of a Marriage

Fifty-seven years. Your low-rise sports car.
Your plaid necktie slung over a tweed shoulder.
Your visor cap, your pipe, a *meerschaum*,

soapy white, hand carved. My scarf, billowing
as we climbed mountain stairs on Hydra.
Your dive from craggy rocks into the Aegean.

The fountain where we met, playing guitars.
Wimoweh. One world. Faces that blurred until
your green eyes creased in corners when you laughed.

And afterwards, the miracle of ordinariness,
the blue wonder of what we'd known before;
sunlight that picked up stains in stainless flatware.

Your well-deep voice that called for decaf coffee.
Dancing soft-shoe to Mahler, listening
in a storm to a storm of timpani.

Bucking winds that augured an icy winter.
Rolling in waves' foam at the shore's edge.
Waking to the fragrance of Russian sage.

Drafts of our lives. Flaming red-orange-yellow
sketches with no overall design,
brushstrokes waiting for a master's hand.

The finished painting that I knew
we'd never own when you lay perfect, complete.

The Rooted Bed

When the medics lifted your lean body
that once loped over hot sand to the sea,
I wanted them to keep you on our bed

resembling one that waited for Odysseus.
He'd carved the bedpost from an olive tree,
alive, still rooted to the earth. For ours,

you'd found a board cut from an oak
and sanded it until it shone like wheat,
a platform for the mattress, unobtrusive

under a quilt, yet there, your handiwork.
In sickness you lay on the rooted bed.
It never moved, just as we stayed put

in one apartment, and heard things rise:
Schubert's Impromptus on a stereo
you'd built, rooted with electric wires

and plugs to be immovable as well,
a pigeon that chirred on the high sill
(you called it a rock dove), until it flew,

Grand Illusion on a video played
over until we memorized the lines.
The bed is still in place. At night without you

I feel it quiver to put down new roots.

The Shirt

Your blue shirt calls me from a closet shelf
above boxes of herringbone caps, sandals,
and a leggy tripod, telescope missing.

I think of Daisy when Gatsby crowed
I've got a man in England who buys me clothes,
flinging them in a color wheel of coral,

lavender, and green, until she sobbed
I'm sad because I've never seen such—
such beautiful shirts. And so today,

tears falling on a massive azure tent,
cuffs big as yawns, its silky cotton
chuffing like a sail in high wind,

I watch the color alter in the light
from sea to sky to ice-blue, and a hint
of ultramarine. And I remember

after we were married—low on funds,
high on our new lives in cramped rooms—
how mornings you'd nuzzle your shirts,

a pride of rainbow checks and tiny stripes
piled like bricks in stacks a dozen high.
I celebrate you, shirt, for long life,

descendant of the world's oldest garment,
a shirt found in an Egyptian tomb,
pleated to flow free. And now I tunnel

through the craterly collar of shirt,
dazzling immortalizer that knows our bodies,
and frays only after we are gone.

Words with the Sea

Groan, sea. Bare your teeth.
  Practice your foamy glissandos.
  Shout as you did to Gauguin
when he painted the woman
  with charcoal hair
in brushstrokes that outlived
  them both.

Roar for the exiled
  Montauk people, who still held rights
  to *fynnes and tales*
of all such whales
  as shall be cast up,
and sang thanks to the god, Moshup,
  for deliverance from hunger.

Crash in the chop of
  a northeast wind, pile up
  heavy stresses. Play back
Whitman's voice when he walked
  on sand declaiming
Hamlet's wonder-wounded lines
  to the waves' applause.

Sea that chews pines
  and spits out language,
  that coughed up seashells
for the head of a Babylonian
  harp shaped like a bull
whose song fused animal,
  man, and god,

rage for my ancestors'
   sadnesses and loves
   they hoisted on ship deck
in wicker suitcases. And hum
   for the raft floated from Havana
on wine barrels, a patched sheet
   for a sail.

Laugh with us, a man and a woman
   kneeling on the shore
   to drip wet sand
and raise a castle—battlements, moat,
   even a crenel window—
then dance over it
   and watch it fall.

Breakers, turn your blank pages
   while I, a stick-figure shadow
   floating diagonally
in bold sun beside you,
   try my voice—
a whisper beneath yours—
   to tell the story.

Meteor

That night the wind-chapped table shouted, *new*:
peaches, bread, still warm, and consecrated
by watery breezes on the shore

of a town whose very name, Springs,
was a carillon that jangled newness.
Talking of ancient ruins with my new friends,

I allowed the wind to rinse regrets,
lights winking miles across the bay,
noiseless, but for surge of waves,

altar-white, before my feet in sand.
And when we turned off lanterns to look skyward
for the Perseids (it was meteor season),

a comet rode queenly across the sky
before it curved and fell. Seeing myself
a speck in the firmament, I remembered

that rock may burn suddenly, blaze into flame
and spin for centuries before it shines
wanting to be remade. Gray rock. The same

that sparkles with mica flecks by day
when breakers slap it clean. Nothing is new.
Nothing alive cannot be altered.

2

Gone

Washington Square, 2020

From my window, I see the world
without us in it: a vacant park,
a silver maple sheltering no reader;

a cherry tree dressed like a bride betrayed,
her wedding cancelled; a dogwood tree
whose whites will fall without regretful eyes.

No baby strollers; no candy wrappers
stuffed in bins; just a sign, NO BICYCLES,
and memories of skateboard pirouettes.

Around us, death: the numbers spin the mind.
Fever dreams. The last breath held, alone.
I hadn't known death had undone so many.

This park reminds us it was once a field
for the unclaimed dead of galloping yellow fever.
Construction workers dug up skeletons

that had lain for years beneath our footsteps.
Death in the hanging elm, a rooted gallows.
Now the clear air, pollution-free, is poison

for walkers, while trees stand stern, immune.
Sad paradox. For comfort, I recall:
Camille Pissarro would have lingered here.

He painted Paris gardens from a window,
having left his island's sprawling shores
for tighter scenes. He gazed at people,

matchsticks from above, in ones and twos.
Below, the park's unlittered paths are mute,
but wait: just now a mournful, prayerful sax,

unseen, from somewhere, unlooses notes,
calls me to the window, and I hear
the sounds I can't imagine days without.

Because

Because, in a wounded universe, the tufts
of grass still glisten, the first daffodil
shoots up through ice-melt, and a red-tailed hawk

perches on a cathedral spire; and because
children toss a fire-red ball in the yard
where a schoolhouse facade was scarred by vandals,

and joggers still circle a dry reservoir;
because a rainbow flaunts its painted ribbons
and slips them somewhere underneath the earth;

because in a smoky bar the trombone blares
louder than street sirens, because those
who can no longer speak of pain are singing;

and when on this wide meadow in the park
a full moon still outshines the city lights,
and on returning home, below the North Star,

I see new bricks-and-glass where the Towers fell;
and I remember my love's calloused hand
soften in my hand while crab apple blossoms

showered our laps, and a yellow rose
opened with its satellites of orange buds,
because I cannot lose the injured world

without losing the world, I'll have to praise it.

Image Worship

Faces on the lid of the Knabe Grand
caught my eye when I tried "The Happy Farmer,"

dreaming of ploughs far from my rutted sidewalks.
Digging, not earth but notes, and neither happy

nor a farmer, I hit wrong keys,
taunted by the metronome. As a distraction,

I stared at smiles in silver frames. War dead.
I never knew them. Heavy-fingered, longing

for their lightness, I saw an uncle waving;
somebody's hell-raiser climbing an oak;

an aunt, a doctor, silk scarf blown in wind.
Suddenly my face appeared among the faces

soon to hide or be interred. The woman's
deep-set eyes in the black-white photograph,

mine in the frame glass, merged, until
the wind lifting her scarf blew through me.

Now, when I stir to brighter images—
a yellow coat, a fawn's sleek arabesque—

I think of photographs, and of Aeneas,
who, in a strange city, stunned by a shrine

with pictures of his own city's destruction,
broken statues, fires, the dead, cried out:

sunt lacrimae rerum: there are tears in things.

Exile

Walking on sand littered with broken shells,
a scallop fan, a whelk cracked on its journey
to shore, I spun around. Far out at sea,

slow at the start, a keening, no, a murmur
as haze cleared and a man grew into sight,
broad shoulders, puffy eyes, looming

above the waves. Ben Webster, soloing.
Holding his tenor sax like a figurehead,
he played in a ghostly breath, a whisper

then a vibrato and a howl in air:
"Time After Time." Time stopped. Years before,
he'd fled to Holland—no work, no money,

racial slurs at home. And now, over the sea's
hiss and churn, comes the unbroken chord,
the tremolo, the weaving five-note phrase,

a low blues filled with shadowed days
missed—on a horn that glisters in the light.

Fireplace Bay

Where are the fires that crackled on this hill?
The leap, the sparks, the urgency of wood smoke,
fires that singed, that heightened conversations

and shadowed sunken jaws. The Montauk people
stoked magenta flames that warned of danger.
The colonists tossed seaweed over fires

for smoke that twisted into bearded clouds
and shouted to the island across the Sound,
food is on its way, smoke-clouds replying:

sheep's wool newly sheared, ready for transport,
and send over clamming rakes from Parson's Smithy.
Speak, fires. Last night a cedar fell

in the downpour, crashing power lines
that need repair. Cell phones fail
without towers nearby; computers sleep

in this speechless neighborhood. I dream of fires
and of a surfman who recounts his catch
in stories that flare up in orange blaze
and circle into smoke. Like words.

Eve Speaks

After you had named *leviathan*,
ziz for great bird, and called out *dissension*
for when the moon glowered at the sun;
creation for beginning, and *expulsion*

for the end, after you gave us *willow*,
thought up *oryx*, and what you tagged *tornado*
sent the olive, God's tree, trembling,
and after symbols—*almonds* for first love,

crocus for lamp glow—you fell silent,
because when you had found labels for *sin*,
archangels, heaven, even (God help you) *God*,

and each new phrase drowned in lion's roar
(or was it divine rage?), you declared *Enough*,
knowing you'd gone too far. Words can't give life
or raise the moon. And still I plead

Say my name, Eve. Say love. Say . . .

Francesca Redux

That day we read no further.

In the beginning, there was the book:
the type, the smell of glue, the grainy paper,
fingertips caressing a stiff spine

that lay flat, the leather cover
crinkled like warm arms, pages fanning open,
stanzas quivering in candlelight,

nouns with open vowels that slid off the tongue,
the wait, the unending sentence with pleasure
delayed. Book, whirl us in wind,

mysterious as marriage, joining words
that had lain apart. After the daily
hoarse falsetto of an alarm clock,

cracked wineglasses and bickering neighbors,
we'll read at night, holding the gilt-edged leaves,
the texts, the bindings that enclose us.

After All

What is it like? You study a hydrangea
that glows lace-white then mauve, and count the whorls
in an oak's huge trunk, split by a hurricane.

You soar with a hawk, not wishing you could fly,
and clamber on the walk in sudden joy.
You linger, seldom glancing at your watch.

You walk to the Hudson River at dawn,
watching a terrier grow out of fog,
and tawny-red bricks that had been blurs

of townhouses the days when you'd whizzed past.
You gaze at them in your own
three-dimensional fullness, unbound,

and you feed the self that you had long neglected
for other selves, the one that knows you best,
and watch the soul burst into sudden bloom,

magenta, like azaleas, and grow larger
when the body lessens.

3

Light in Genoa

Irma Brandeis, my teacher at Bard

1

Some things come clear only in purest light,
in Montale's Italy, near Genoa,
where the altering sea shimmers at moonrise.

I thought I knew her at the hilltop college,
her black hair clasped like ecstasy held back,
often alone; on walks, she'd name the trees,

asking an oak unanswerable questions.
Green eyes shone sapphire when she spoke of Dante's
doomed lovers, circling on the wind.

I never guessed that she was one of them.
But here, gasping at a fresco's angels,
with sidelong glances that invite the soul,

and at erotic sculptures in a cemetery—
(if the dead could speak, they'd moan in passion
I imagined a rose in her unbound hair.

2

I knew they had been lovers from his poems
that ring of bellflowers quivering in wind,
phallic cypresses—and there she is,

his Beatrice of the journey that ironically
brought her to Italy. Seeking Dante's hell
she met Montale, thought his humor dull,

his face unfortunate—but not his lines.
So it began, their fire: an incandescent
light at sunset; a balcony in Genoa;

a rocky path, its stones set like mosaics;
swims in a cove. Five years. Then came the shouts
that shattered speech, when shutters slammed

and eyes shut in the sea town's ochre houses.
Nineteen thirty-eight. The Fascist laws.
She left, and just in time. She was a Jew.

3

Montale, hear me now. Life, you once wrote,
is watching a stone wall with cracked glass slivers
stuck on top. One day I stumbled on

a wall like that, high on a mountain terrace,
and knew that you could never risk the climb—
or join her, leaving these gold hours.

Instead, you sent remorse, and married one
who swore suicide if you kept your Clizia,
as you called her, for the water nymph

turned sunflower to watch Apollo,
the sun god whom she loved, in vain. And Clizia
turned into Irma, sunflower to moonflower,

in tailored suits. She never spoke of you.
Only in Genoa, I've understood
that through smart bombs and misery you'd seen her

the way this fire lily breaks through rock
at the sea's edge, in the unfractured light
that is, perhaps, the hero of your story.

Moment in Rapallo

Your mind went double, like these two brass doorknobs
that lead into your house. I tried one. Locked.
Years past you had unlocked my mind to hear

language charged with meaning, and to feel
that sense of sudden growth, and as for rhythm,
the churn, the loom,

                    the spinning wheel, the oar.

An old scribe quotes King Solomon:
God created our organs in duplicate,
two hearts, two minds.

                    For you, two loyalties.

No pure homage, then, these lines go double
for the mind that battened on division
as it winced and stirred:

                    I pictured you

descending from your attic to the harbor
where triangle sails fishermen call lateens
called back ancient boats,

                    the past made new.

There you were, in your seaside caffè,
listening to wave-sounds while declaiming
in two languages;

arranging concerts

for your double-love, a violinist
playing Bach in praise beyond division.
I'd seen you that way.

But now, suddenly,

my hand on an unyielding yellow doorknob,
fiery through the mist, after a storm
had sunk harbor boats

like your once-buoyant

mind, capsized, split, at once I see:
the fascist salute; the love turned sour;
the right turned wrong,

the language charged

with meaning suddenly meaningless, degraded,
madness denied at first, the mind's locked door.
I pulled my hand back,

fearing the brass might,

as in gilt statues, rub off in my palm.

Alive and Well: Tomb Sculptures in the Staglieno Cemetery

Genoa, Italy

1 ANGEL

So this is death, lifelike in marble
and unconsoling, on a merchant's tomb.
No man with a scythe, no man at all,
but her, slim-hipped in an airy gown

nipped at the waist; on the high breast
one hand rests, the slender fingers
limp, waiting to beckon or direct,
come-hither lips—barbed wings.

The eyes translucent, clear lakes
you want to fathom, but the gaze
says, I don't want to be known
or understood. Angel of cold passion.

Angel of sex and death: essential answers
hidden in one vamp. When I pass by,
she turns to follow. Death, you terrify—
just as you lure me with a knowing glance.

2 WIDOW

I know her by the pleated satin dress,
hair in a bun, the hesitation
as she lifts the sheet, letting air in,
astonished, peering into darkness—

(what will she find there?)—at her husband's body,
suddenly altered. Questions run through her:
dare she kiss the lips now growing colder?
Can he hear her? Leaning awkwardly,

loath to leave him, venturing a touch,
she asks now, why him? In unending silence,
she clings to precise details for an answer,
side-glancing at the unmade bed, the high

pile of cushions falling from their place.
I know her by my husband's silver watch
that hasn't stopped. The still warm belly.
The pearl pajama button on the terrace.

3 DREAMER

Clerics opposed her installation here,
so close to rosaries, hands clasped in prayer.
Officials said: a travesty of holiness,
pagan, impious. Other slurs unclear.

What was it? Not the lips about to part,
the mouth to speak, the tousled hair,
the robe that slides down a bare shoulder,
curvy hips -- those were the sculptor's art.

Nor was it her calm perch, dreaming, not dead.
The dream, though: those three ovals in her hand,
seemingly blossoms, are poppy pods
formed after flowering, from whose sticky substance

opium is drawn. Demeter in grief
over her daughter's fate, would sip the stuff
to soothe her loss. At the Staglieno,
sexy is fine. Is life. Addiction, no.

4 MARIA FRANCESCA

Eyes shut, as in elation more than death,
the legs straining to spring from their marble bed,
a sheet slipped to reveal the nude young breasts,
spool waist. Not the shattered body found

in a car crash, fingers severed and flung,
this likeness is perfect, shaped, from a photograph
—notice the glow, the urge to speak, to laugh.
Unlike some broken statues, hinting at arms

and phalluses, she gleams in all her parts.
Alone but not alone. Her man in marble
bends to kiss her and clutch her thigh,
not in lust but in finality.

I know the scene. Your body fixed but yearning
to move again. I'm moving now in scattered
pieces, over miles and time. Free neither
to finish the task of life nor to abandon it.

5 STRUGGLE

If these stones were flesh, you'd hear their cries:
Death, blank-faced and stiff, and a lithe woman
who won't be taken by those tigery claws
without a kick, a blow, a fierce objection.

She bends, covered waist down in see-through tulle,
actually marble carved to look ethereal
with the same mallet, calipers, and chisel
the sculptor used to shape rock into muscle.

Waist up exposed, but raging, unafraid.
The work unfinished, dinners to order,
dresses to try on, letters to write.
When, that last night, you called for slacks and blazer
from your sickbed, I watched the pull-away,
the savage, sun-driven though futile, fight.

6 WOMAN IN SUNLIGHT

Carved in marble, white now gone to grime,
mottled, soot-blotched, smeared, with blurred letters,
a lithe woman reclines in a gauzy nightdress,
curved from substantial hip to supple ankles,

but for the cross she holds, I'd say in languor.
Stare at her, stare until you see lean hands
open to grasp at air, feet kick to dance,
silk hair unfold like a billowing scarf,

and linger for the long intake of breath.
I want to move inside the blackened stone
and find a spark that flares up into blaze

and flashes like sunbeams—to dazzle
with tales of what it could be like to walk
out of my weathered body. Clean. Alive.

Italy

Sexless angels? Not these fiery dancers
on tower walls. In church, they wink at those
who light candles and pray under a knee
slipped out of an angel's robe, chiseled to flow.

Hardly androgynous, seraphim lure.
A woman slinks beside a saucy cherub.
On this bridge, Ponte Sant'Angelo,
stone angels stand in flimsy gowns slit high.

I've read that once an angel lighted here
to trumpet the end of a deadly plague;
now erotic angels sing the end
of cold indifference. Heavenly ministers,

unpuritanical, fan out enormous wings
and forgive even my careless loves.

4

Ascension

That morning, in the Church of the Ascension
on lower Fifth, once a sanctuary
for bonnets and top hats, I had a vision

of clipped pines, bamboo, a Kyoto garden.
Odd. In La Farge's painting above the altar,
Christ rises from the dead while his disciples

gaze heavenward, and angels swim in air,
two and two and two, draped in white silk.
But why bamboo? Perhaps I had a reason.

La Farge, his marriage ended, brushes dry,
went to Japan and gasped when he found Fuji.
He saw the mountaintop float like a god,

loom over him, and fade. At once renewed,
he painted Christ rising from the hills
to heaven's kingdom. And when I looked

long enough, the Mount of Olives
changed into Mount Fuji's snowcapped cone,
immobile, while a stream flows, an image

of what Lao Tsu called life's stillness and motion.
Now, in the Church of the Ascension,
I praise all things that soar and make a crowd

glance skyward: a wave of white thistledown,
an egret's dangling legs in flight; a siren-red
balloon; snow wafting high; a Buddhist's moon;

La Farge's Christ that turns into the Great Buddha
shimmering in bronze; and after that
Mohammed's horse; Elijah's chariot

let fly above the altar. I'll be there,
gazing impiously—unless
that is what sacred is, the work, the looking up,
                    the wonder.

Agony in the Garden

Oil on canvas, Giovanni Bellini
National Gallery, London

No garden,   not
in the leafy sense.

No Eden,   certainly,
just high treeless rock.

See me now,   no god,
a man, afraid.   Friends,

or so they swore, loved as they
could. Now   I'm hunted,

they fake sleep. How can I—
can I run from

betrayal?   Is this a cup
of poison   or salvation?

A prickly   altar for prayer:
granite with   knifeblade edges,

and here's no   ordinary
first light. Clouds' underbellies,

silver at dawn,   bode lightning.
Or a shock   of angels.

Tell me which   it will be.
Pray for them   pray

for stillness,   pray
to do right.

My sweat runs red
freely,   like blood

streaming,   thigh gashed
on a razory rock.

Look there,   far away,
flies swarming in sight?

No, soldiers wandering
over a bridge,   at ease,

harmless.   Almost
restful.   At rest.

At last.
Arrest.

Geniza

The old Egyptian merchants stored their rubble
in a geniza, the synagogue's attic
for papers that might contain God's name.

In my mind I sort those grimy fragments.
Junk, but holy. A bill for camels.
A marriage contract. The price of silk.

When to have sex. When not to have sex.
Someday I'll feed my drafts to a geniza
that pants to eat lines crossed out and restored,

fire in a tulip's glaze, scribbled-on road maps,
a list of Indian spices, a love letter
signed with an unremembered name.

My tattered notes will lie with holy lines
like Yannai's phrase about the burning bush,
fire that devours fire. His life was known

less than his wonder, which was kept
for burial in sanctified ground.
If one poem is a message in a bottle

destined to be found, those messages
wait, written on vellum, dank, foul-smelling,
in rock-hard words that will not give up life.

Still Lifes,

alive. No people here, but objects speak
of the Dutch merchant who stands invisible
behind one painting, smoking a clay pipe,

newly prosperous, proud of his table,
and of his country's new free trade.
His things tell me of a life unfinished,

half-devoured: half-wheels of cheese, cut apple,
succulent oysters on shiny half-shells.
And in another, a porcelain dish

the lady bought and carried home; the lemon peel—
oh yes, the lemon-peel—a standby
in the Dutch family, pebbly yellow skin

that twists in air, mouth-puckering bitter taste.
Things chatter about parties interrupted,
lives in progress: the silver tray

upended; broken glass on linen; watch
stopped, pried open, its works exposed.
Possessions, bodiless yet full of being,

livelier for being used, half worn,
their scars glinting in warm light, exist
in dailiness made sacred by regard.

The Lost Explorers

Give me the lost explorers, the last-seens,
gone missings, vanished-in-fog, no wreckage found,
with names that ring with danger, like Uemura
and Crozier, or rhyme with awe, like Fawcett.

I'll take the one who feels exile at home
and breathes deep on departures, who would quit
leather recliners for a matchbox plane
to soar in, clutching a windblown chart,

or one who drives a dogsled through the snow's
blank pages, the way unmarked by tracks
or wheel-ruts, and the life an open question.
Names echo like the last notes of a fugue.

Watch them stir to chatter in hissing consonants
and growls of a new language; dare them to travel
across the world's time zones until they find
extra days, past and future. I'll cheer for

listeners to wind song, losing balance
only to right themselves (who hasn't walked on,
steadier, once lost?), just as I write this
with broken compass and no GPS.

Crime in the Conservatory Garden

Alone, afraid in Central Park that year,
the local crime rate climbing like a fever,
I stepped from gray-green trees to a living Oz,

my sandals emerald slippers in a garden
planted with bosomy balloon flowers
and flirty narcissi. High on lilacs,

I angled through a vacant walkway.
Loud steps followed, scuffing the pavement.
Tense now, looking urgently at asters

bordering the path, expecting to hear,
Give me your wallet, and to answer, *yes,*
but not my life, please. I turned back.

Staring at my stare, he uttered, pointing:
They call these creepy things wisteria.
Nice, but go to the garden in the Bronx,

botanical, they call it, large enough
to fit in six like this one. In that brief
fellowship, trying to forget the walker

beaten by strangers only a walk from there,
I joined him, basking in the luminous coneflowers
of an imperfect world. Letting go

of a maple's trunk, I raised my hand
to give him a mint stem I'd snipped, illegally.
He offered me a stolen fern. Partners we were

in the only misdemeanors there that day.

Greenwich Village Street Talk

Step gingerly before these brownstone houses,
the color Edith Wharton called a cold
chocolate sauce. A rectangle warns, DANGER.

FLYING WORDS. Henry James hurls epithets,
labeling Whitman's latest *arrant prose*
and damns high buildings that hide the past.

Where names are cut in brass, listen for voices:
lovers of Edna St. Vincent Millay
deride her passion for new loves, new sins

to fill new lines. Her own confession, *all
atoning mine*. I hear *all stoning mine*—
and yes, if words can stone, walk at your peril.

A bar, long gone, still bristles with opinion,
and the dead argue, rattling iron bars
of the Jewish graveyard, while a street sign brags

West Fourth/West Fourth, each vying for top place.
Other ghosts howl, these criticize,
hissing until a siren drowns their words.

An open door is an eye that sees my jeans
unfashionable for dinner. Through that door,
another door. I'll ring—another day.

Right now I'll turn the corner for a getaway.

Erratic

Erratic: Latin, from errare, to wander

The rock outside my door is called erratic:
a wanderer, picked up by a glacier
millions of years ago. Pocked, battered, scarred,

with a blank stare by day, it glowers
under a full moon. Inscrutable,
and, by definition, unpredictable,

a monument missing the usual plaque
(an Indian well stood here, a battle
fought), its history is cut in grooves:

cracked off a mountain, riding an ice floe
that, like a lover, left it to spin wild.
Erratic, you sit sunken in mud,

an exile, with the same battling desires
that rule my life: to change or to hold fast.
With frown lines in your granite face, you claim,

it's not that I came to this but how,
fixed to the spot but still churning inside,
dreaming of the trip with your icy lover,

trout leaping under frozen rivers,
people chanting over sacred stones.
You are the true explorer, one who quit

bedrock attachments to roll along
new roads that would reveal the granite self,
now my companion traveler in place.

The Wind Game

Another hot day, late sun, boats becalmed,
windless, wildflowers hangdog on their stems.

The sloop was out, sail forward, with no motor.
We stood on shore watching the mate's daughter

writing in sand, unfazed by our alarm.
She asked what we were doing, lanky figures,

our towels draped like prayer shawls, searching water.
Waiting for wind, a man said with fake cheer,

hedging to distract her, masking his fear,
drew breath and blew. A woman sucked in air,

as in a game. Soon we were all hard-breathing,
blowing dream trumpets, wafting imagined storms.

The child puffed out plump cheeks, mimicking thunder.
Shadows gathered. There was muffled talk

of launching the dinghy for the lost sloop
in hope of rescuing the girl's father.

Suddenly wind rose, whipped swamp reeds,
and tossed green-yellow flags. A white sail.

Sighs. Laughter. The child spoke: *That was good.*
What will we do next? as she stalked driftwood

to carve her name in letters that will last
just for the day. How could we tell her

it was not the will that plumps the sails
of sloops and brings them home to beach on sand?

That Summer

Joy began with a cerulean sky
and breaths of grass, sweeter than subway odors.
My mind was playing over the warm hard runs

of Sonny Rollins on tenor sax,
in rhythm with the roll of a wooden pier,
brash kids beside me, gleaming wet in sun.

Urgent yet serene, his tones kept hidden
what I'd read of his early addiction.
Crime, jail. Overcome. No lasting harm.

Lifted, perhaps, by someone's sturdy arms.
Savoring the single notes and lulls,
risking the wild delight of his "Gazelle,"

I knifed into the lake, seemingly tranquil,
limpid, with emerald weeds. A sudden whirl
pulled me around. I swam, steering upward,

and turned—the wrong way. Blue pain. My head
hit the deck's underside, no space to breathe.
I thought the tide would suck me down to mud.

No, someone saw. Sturdy arms dragged me up,
changed, knowing how close bliss was to dread
and how it must have been to yell for help,

hear no sound, and scream through your horn instead.

The Vow

That day I stepped gingerly with my father
playing father (actors played their parts)
down the blue-carpeted aisle to be wed

—or tried for treason. A skeletal pianist
fingered a funeral march, hitting wrong notes.
We passed Mom in a dress sizes too large

she'd bought to play the mother-of-the-bride.
My own tight bodice pinched as I gasped for breath,
bound for a new life, knowing the old would do.

I glanced upward at friends playing hope,
my roses drying brown as I neared an altar
set too high and built of rotting pine.

My father gave this woman, me, to some
imposter who would want me to be faithful
as Ruth, which meant, I supposed, to follow

my mother-in-law, whither she goest.
Yes, I wanted this, but want is a moment
in a long sentence without punctuation.

What if like some birds I could not sing
in captivity? Would it be, I pleaded,
security or maximum security?

Divorce would disappoint my grandmother
crying here (for joy?) in silk chiffon.
And then at last I saw him, the one

who wasn't playing anyone, his eyes
hazel, shining like aggies in first light—
and I said *yes, of course, I will, I will.*

Cinderella

I was fifteen, too thin, and six feet tall
with outsize feet, though still believing
in a glass slipper. Until that night

at a high school dance, when the teacher barked,
Every girl must toss one shoe on the mound
for a boy to choose and take its owner.

I gazed at shells in suede, in patent leather,
swirly, with curvy insteps, ice pick heels,
and tucked my flat-heeled sandal under them,

nails clawing through the heel I'd hammered off
to stand a half-inch lower. They had said
someday you'll be glad you're tall. But someday

was tonight. I hoped that some odd suitor
would see beyond the shoe to me myself.
Boys hunted the heap. I saw my sandal

left alone, intruder in the ring
before the teacher poked it with a pointer,
watched it squirm, and hoisted it high:

Whose shoe is this? No need to ask again.
I ran home barefoot in the rain, skidding
on slick pavement, resolved to find my way
that night and after. Never mind the prince.

Moon Plant

Satiny moons shine out and summon memory:
an egret's luminous wing, your dinghy's sail.
Moon plant, *lunaria rediviva,*
a weed unplanned, with persistent roots.

Peel off the shell and find transparent screens,
the filmy parchment for suibokuga,
a Japanese art: brush dipped in sumi ink
and stroked so that no wrong line

could cut through. No second chances.
I hear moons ring like silver dollars
stamped with a rare promise:

In God We Trust. Airy moons endure,
stripped to their naked skins and vulnerable
though still intact. Each a blank screen. For hope.

A Love Supreme

The man who gave up drugs for God
raised a soprano sax, now a ram's horn
calling us to confess, now a muezzin's

summons, now a gospel benediction.
Arpeggios gave way to squawking tones,
staccato barks praised ugliness as beauty.

My date nudged me. *Why can't he stand still?*
Why so loud? I can't hear the words.
Coltrane stood alone, on the massive stage

of the old movie house on Second Avenue,
and soloed. I heard the past, not his
and not America's, but the Creation,

and as noisy: a sea monster roared,
elephants ran wild, a hawk cried out,
sun and moon raged to be the stronger light.

So that was what it came to, Love Supreme.
He played the present -- grit, road kill,
street kill -- shrieking like a gull

as it drops to feed from a cracked shell
then rises up on scarf-like wings and flies.
Silence. The solo over, my date grumbled,

Squeaks, screams, those manic wails, and razz.
He left. I shrugged, and stayed for the long flight.

Dr. John

Stage name of Malcolm John Rebennack, Jr.

Remember strutting high in the night air
at Mardi Gras. Wearing the Voodoo gown,
silky emerald, bones and crosses clinking,

hands racing on keys. Remember losing
the beat. Losing time, and time was all,
like watching your shadow fade at dusk.

Trying to call down the beat, *Shallow water,*
yo ma-ma, hu-tunnay two-way pock-a-way,
accents weak as a rain chant in a storm

outshouted by thunder, pleas unheard.
Drinking cure-alls with jimson weed, stroking
embroidered amulets, scrapping your name,

Rebennack, for Dr. John, a caster of spells
who wielded snakes. Invoking Voodoo queens,
lifting the doll, rubbing the healing stone,

and when the charms failed, drugs, jail,
where you watched days merge in mist, out of time,
eyes blurred, unfocused. Now from a high window

in the detox ward, you see a woodchuck waddle
then run to miss car wheels. Turning back,
you eye the lock box, drugs, dreams inside.

To pry it open would mean jail again.
Gonna take my gang on Mardi Gras day,
say mighty coody-fiyo get out of the way.

Half notes pound. You lie back in bed
and twitch awake, under a hawk's claw
on a low flight, blackjack, handcuffs, the law.

No talons. Instead, a woman's hand, an orderly's,
tapered fingers open on a ball,
saggy, pocked skin, color of sunset.

You bite into a tangerine, unpeeled,
and feel sweet-sour trickle down your throat.
Cool dawn. Then fire, as when you heard the beat

that first day in your father's music store,
and went out under stars, singing, *Yo-mama,*
hu-tunnay two-way pock-a-way.

It was good. And on another Sunday
in a crowded ward, you heard the beat.

El Greco's Vision of Saint John

Dazzled by silk robes they've cast aside
in colors of sunflower petals, leaves
green-gold in spring's first bloom, and wine-red roses

I see the saints writhing as they lunge
for plain robes they would wear to the highest throne.
Heaven threatens. Cherubs plummet

as I gasp, hoping their mothy wings will hold.
El Greco's fire-forced painting is unfinished
like the saints' indefinite ascension.

Torn canvas. A fragment, meant for an altarpiece.
How the mind, my mind, longs for completeness
and paints the Lamb to go with Saint John's vision,

not there before, and yet its absence glowed.
Now in the gallery, I step aside
for a wheelchair: a young woman, her eyes

arcing to light-bleached colors in the painting,
fragment though it is. She lifts her arms
to the dead, and all I see are hands,

hers, hands of the artist, hands of souls
extended, reaching across four centuries
touching like a sycamore's branches

across a road. Hands that tell me holiness
is actually unwhole. Perfection
is never the end-all, not even in heaven.

6

Blizzard

Why am I here in this stunning tranquility?
Pines are not pines, their branches under down;
harlequin trunks and hooded zinnias
(or whatever, in disguise) ignore me

as I watch millions of six-pointed flakes
drift into a mass, hiding the road.
Exile begins with the unfamiliar:
now a missed elm, now words that fail.

In the windowpane my face is gone.
My body's lighter. I've lost my name.
Feathers fly, those silvery things out there
must be birds. Unless they're angels,

singing as the wind sings, out of tune.
Silence now. Blank sky, the car a bear
asleep. It's dark at four, time to trudge out
watchful, and search for anything—a stone, a twig,

a root—unchanged.

The Rainbow Sign

God gave Noah the rainbow sign,
No more water, the fire next time.

Like cotton candy, spun of cloud and air,
two ribbons slipped from yardage under the earth
spooling out brightness past a sea of shipwrecks.

Yesterday's hurricane spun through the village,
shattering panes, burying cars in sand,
splintering a neighbor's wooden pier,

its piles still jutting up like broken molars,
wrenching wires, screaming of loss.
Blackout. Our faces flushed in candlelight,

we watched nerve-ends of lightning shock the windows
and questioned wall shadows for predictions.
Today, the rainbow sign, God's weather news:

The waters shall never again become a flood
to destroy all flesh.
                    Relief? Well, promises,
the longing for belief that comes in language

clear as in a child's coloring book:
violet, blue, green, yellow, orange, red,
upgraded here to lilac, cobalt, clay,

new life green, wheat yellow, and carmine.
Rainbow, heal the world with sudden light.
Let us drive into bars of tinted gauze

then hide indoors until the fire next time.

Bald Angel

At last I've found the angel I can wrestle,
not just a throne who might fly off at dawn
but a master of takedown holds and grapples.

This bald eagle shrugs on a craggy post,
praying, if prayer is close attention,
dead still, except for darting agate eyes

surveying prey, or else in observation.
Not hairless but white-headed, with huge wings
tucked behind, power held in check,

and a fierce frown. Now he stares in silence
like one of the exalted seraphim
while seagulls, lesser guardians, shriek hosannas.

March now, and the sea winds are too calm.
The air is tranquil, promising warm breezes.
Perhaps he's come not to bring rough tides

but to amaze me: clutch me by the shoulder
with yellow graspers, rip open my eyes,
and lift off loudly, bitching, cursing, blessing.

Don't!

Hard to believe her boasts, the old woman,
daughter of a Pope that never was

or to know why Candide, fraught with mistakes,
all wisdom failed, must ask her what to do.

How she rattles on about disasters:
captured by pirates, stripped, run through with daggers,

and yet she claims, baring a shoulder:
A hundred times I've wanted to kill myself

but always I loved life more.
That I believe. Of course, there's reason

to quit: the broken-elevator drop from love,
the fall from affluence and influence,

the slump after betrayal, fooled by lies.
But hear me out, sad friend, and then resolve

to leap from no high roof, never OD,
use your Santoku knife to cut sashimi,

wander in this field of fresh strawberries
and pick boxfuls, until the bright red juice

not blood, stains your hands. Serve them with wine;
if any are left for jam, break out a pan,

turn up the gas—not for the deadly element
but fire, gaze at the blue/red ring of flame

and your existence is, will be, the fire.

Fallen Poets

As houselights dim, we mourn death's latest haul
with Verdi's Requiem. Grant them eternal rest
—and hear no rest, not when those drums boom fire.
Menacing chants, sobs, moans, shatter the calm.

The dead ooze through the string section, and roar,
hard as the conductor, arms in air,
waves them away. Shouts blare from the horns,
onstage and off, ranting, *Too soon,*

more work to come. They fill the trombones,
rattle the oboes, frighten the baritone.
Now I expect a down-there choir to steam
up from hell, sing out over the brass

and drown the cellos. That is what anger is.
And God will hush his calmer seraphim
at their meek *Agnus Deis*, to hear his frenzied
men and women cry out *Dies irae*—

day of *their* wrath. Rage for the singing dead.

Ballade for the Duke of Orleans

I die of thirst here by the fountainside,
and others dared to emulate that rasp
in tones of wonder, showing how we gasp
like fish on land for what cannot be ours.
In our time, Richard Wilbur cast his lot
for first prize, followed by John Hollander,
and Mona Van Duyn. And I know how it is
to live in gold imagination, not
accept the facts, ever dissatisfied,
to die of thirst here by the fountainside.

The morning sun shines on a field of reeds
gone gray, nodding like prophets on their stalks;
all else is green despite the weeks-long dread
of dryness. Now the neighbor woman talks
of weather, too-little rain, too chilly
for June, her back turned on new daffodils
and on a branch that has an oversized
hard-on, and bows to scoop up air and rise.
She speaks of better times. Ever dissatisfied,
she'll die of thirst here by the fountainside.

My workroom is a chapel. I'll confess
to seeing parched bamboo through emerald glass.
My pen writes praise shadowed by recent dead,
seeing a cardinal over emerald grass
bright as a basting-stitch in scarlet thread,
hostas as yet uneaten by deer, and, yes,
redbuds circling an orange rose like planet-rings.
To hold back beauty, stay with your imaginings,

with the mind's eye, not the eye, or otherwise,
you'll die of thirst here by the fountainside.

Your Grace: pocket your cash. I'll take Coltrane's
prayerful low notes that, falling, rise, like rain
over high waves, and not decide
to die of thirst there by the fountainside.

Letter from Nicaragua

In July, 1979, the Nicaraguan government, under General Anastasio
Somoza's leadership, fell after fighting between national soldiers
and rebel forces.

"Querida Grace: The Lake is phosphorescent,
a freshwater sea of sharks the Indians
called Cocibolca, lair of the great snake,
chuckles under the wharf. Calabash trees

have star-shaped leaves, ceibas wear cotton ruffs.
Yes, I'm alone, but when I laugh my cove
fills with echoes. [Signed with loops that leaned
like windblown trees], Con Abrazos, Pablo."

Suddenly formal, "Pablo Antonio Cuadra."
His words, the first I had since gunfire
shone like the chalk-white ceiba tree his ancestors,
mavericks also, named "the exile's shelter."

A love letter from one I'd never met
but knew from his lines that glowed like burning coals.
Born of law-makers, he broke social laws
to live with fishermen and sail the Lake.

I'd heard they carried Pedro Joaquin,
his murdered cousin, in a via crucis
through mud roads. Days past, at La Prensa,
both railed at censorship. He would be next.

For Pedro's wake, they trekked in from the fields
hog-raisers, farmers, smiths, from moonlit slips
scribbling on the sky with hand-dipped candles.
I cried out Run! and tucked his letter

into its wrapper. Late FM news:
The death toll rises as the city falls
to rebels. But by morning, rebels ruled.
Rank opposites, the same. Again, mass slaughter.

The tyrant gone, the rescuer took his chair,
warlord to lords of war. Before word came,
I saw Pablo in my mind's eye, safe,
writing under a cacao tree

in red-yellow bloom, on Lake Nicaragua.
Not a lake. An ocean. Endless waves. Freshwater,
yet filled with sharks and shad. His sweet sea.
In hiding, his lines blazed with faith

that women who carried baskets of hemp
and fishermen who tied slipnets to anchors
knew ropes had strength to bind people in peace.
Now, where birds that shit fear in water

Recover in air order, freedom, song,
He walks with Medardo, maker of nets,
And with Pascasio, the one-armed sailor.
With canticles of praise gasped under thunder,

Pablo, your voice fills sails. You prod horizons,
Eyes kindling the sea, waiting for dawn.

The Worst

The worst is not
So long as we can say, "This is the worst."
       —*Edgar, in* King Lear

No, not the worst, not if it can be named.
Say sorrow. Say disaster. Say no cure
for the cared-for or the caregiver.

Tell grief in images, in heavy stresses,
and you will know it's worse, but not the worst:
Weak legs will stride and fall, then stride again.

In darkness, verbs breed sight, in sickness, laughter.
Nouns don't console, though they cut deeper,
in hard hours, for the sea smell, for the weightlessness

of a cormorant wing-flapping on a buoy,
for how on a leaking dory men haul bass,
and ride over shipwrecks on a choppy sea.

The Jetty

When it came clear your good heart had gone bad,
I walked to the sea for stones, the weight,
the pull of them, the scrubbed squeak in my pocket
of moon-yellows, whites, and pale merlots.

Far off, unbroken breakers grumbled over
the doctor's supposition: easy death,
seemingly wrong, because your heart still quickened
to skies that went on uninterrupted

over a jetty made to check wild currents.
Suddenly I knew it would be like this,
not with a splash that recedes to surge again,
but with a white explosion against boulders.
That one day in sleep I'd reach for you
and close on air, my mind gone white
                           against flat stones.

Caregiver

Caretaker, career
                    steward, sworn lover,

companion, recorder
                    of heart rates, if heart

can be rated;
                    unresting, reminder

of amethyst hours.
                    Carrier of cheer,

custodian of someone
                    no one can own;

head manager, planner,
                    quick to the answer,

unfazed, of the phone,
                    never alone—

stitched to the other,
                    a secret sharer,

and, like the sinner
                    condemned to a circle

of howlers in hell,
                    hearing one call.

Waiting Room

The surgeon had said cured—but for a time.
White-robed attendants coasting like seabirds,
I wandered out of "Waiting" to the chapel
where a man in a death's head t-shirt

crouched, forehead to carpet, facing east.
Alone (or possibly in unison?)
I mumbled thanks. Amen to his Aneen.
Days afterward, recovery on an island

where time slow-danced like waves, the sand bar
set like the keyboard of an unseen pianist
who mingled jazz beats with symphonic swells.
On shore, a palm tree wound its fronds

like clock hands. As that day swam back
and harbor lights blinked on, I thought of how
time that pummels rocks, switchblade in teeth,
and dressed to kill, could heal.

Survival in the Woods

After the chapel prayers, I went to the woods
for clearance, clearings in trees, clearness
of mind. For sunlight on the ground
strained through leaves. Dazed by loss,

I came for images of things that last:
catbrier that hooks tendrils into bark.
Poplars that soar unbroken, hushed in rain,
and high-branched oaks, wind's roarers

that toss their topmost leaves like dice
in a game of chance, taking the odds on danger.
The Baal Shem Tov, carrying sorrow
for those in pain, built fires in the woods,
sat balanced on a splintered log, and when
prayer didn't come, he'd tell a story.

: : :

On this land the colonists thought Satan,
masked as a Mohawk, lurked among the maples,
so Satan hurled dank images at me:
white grubs, possums, blind worms, and, slimier,

water snakes from under the brown leaf carpet,
star-nosed moles, onyx-and-purple slugs,
all crawlers. As I stared they glittered
in the dark woods, and I remembered brightness.

Once I'd misread a museum plaque, Pissarro's
"Edge of the Woods" for "Edge of the World."
He'd left wide shores to paint tight woods in France,
finding new freedom in limitation.
At the world's edge, slender vines cling
to ancient alders. Life holds on to life.

: : :

Oaks claim their dead. Poets, young suicides,
are here grown into pines. But claiming life,
Jews lived in the woods, evading guards,
crouched in holes, starved, drinking from rivers.

A branch snaps. I remember my origin,
not as I had thought, in my tall city
of sidewalk squares, but in the forest
where new shoots break through dry-leaf cover,

where there are no full-stops, only motion
that leads me on, where the trail before me
slopes to blankness, and I land unharmed.
My name is Schulman, mine by a long marriage,
though I had another name at birth:
Waldman, woodman, survivor in the woods.

Springs Song

My beloved has gone into his garden,
we read on Passover, this one in Springs,
a greeny town, to mark the holiday

of probing questions and indifferent answers.
Why is this night different from all others,
the ritual begins, and my mind strays:

why leaf through the steamy Song of Songs
about the slender neck of someone's lover
while a child looks blank? Better to ask,

Where has my beloved gone? Into his garden,
his ashes marked by a stone circle
under a beech tree that sheds no leaves,

not even in winter. White-gold bellflowers
ring their short hours, daylilies live their days;
chrome-yellow dandelions pock a green lawn.

Soon the forsythia will lose its blaze.
In fall the golds will hide in winter's sentences,
visible, invisible. In Hebrew, love and death

sound almost alike, *ahav, mavet.*
Outside, a goldfinch flicks the feeder
scattering seed over stones. Inside,

the wheelchair, once a racer, is dead still
in what I've called and call our living room.

Year's End

Icy wind. The wait for the car to start
while the real wait is for the year to end.
Perhaps it will close with arrival,

like the affair that ends in a long marriage.
Arrival. Advent. *Veni Creator Spiritus,*
Come Creative Spirit, in the Mahler Symphony

we heard, with its endless beginnings.
To come. To come back. This year's in fragments
like the torn ticket stubs I pocketed

hoping to hear the Mahler whole again.
Here among bare oaks, the juniper's
needles still cling when berries fall.

Perseverance. The art of going on
while carrying the past. The Persian horse
in the new carpet, the sea turtle

that swims for miles with an ancient eye;
and here, the snowy egret, a white cloud
flickering through a wall of cedars,

feet flowing behind like a bridal train,
braving frost, the head thrown back in flight.
Soon it will stab minnows with a probing beak

when it finds the marsh, lower blond feet
and slide down air to a new landing.

The Letting Go

1 WAITING MUSIC

Evenings I watch the junipers turn gray
waiting for the peppermill grind
of your key in the lock, the door's groan,
the arrow of light, the spin of leaves, your car

crunch gravel and light up the ivy
you'd sunk in earth. Spring, when the garden's flush
with gold—dandelion, buttercup—the finch
taunts, dead means dead, not just away

investigating dendritic cells
to cure diseases. Your Bach CD stalls
downtempo. I grow older. Hear my plea.
Had you sailed the river in a storm
I'd have worn boots and trampled out at dawn
to meet you, as far as Cho-Fu-Sa.

2 THE SECOND LINE

You knew the odds on death, your practiced mind
reeled with the diagnosis, *Cardiac
Failure, Stage Four*. And still you planned
Philharmonic nights, one of them jazz,

whose pair of tickets sears my calendar.
Go, New Orleans jazzmen, hit a low note
for the man who craves your flourishes.
Celebrate. Start up the second line,

trumpet and snare drum. Play it hot, up-tempo.
Let the street crowd amble, strut, kick high.
Open the scarlet petals of umbrellas
and spin with dancers as the band wails.

There you are, foot-tapping. In silver light
you listen to a man in a silk top hat
who shouts: "Rejoice. Another soul gone home."
The saints go marching in to raise a life.

3 BENEDICTUS

"How will you confess your disbelief
to the Highest Judge?" I asked,
science your faith, your candles microscopes,
your psalters vials. I went on. "Bertrand Russell

thought he'd say, 'Belief? I wasn't given
enough evidence.' And you?" The quick reply,
"Belief? I wasn't given ANY evidence."
Of course, no proof. No quantitative measures.

So I persisted: "What of renewal?
Spring's first snowdrop celebrating God's
and the god's return?" "No, that's biology,
the plant's roots left behind." I paused, defeated.

Bach alone got through. The car radio
sent contrapuntal strains washing over us,
waves crested with messages
if we listened hard, then got sucked back

to a sea that widened endlessly. The tenor sang,
Benedictus qui venit in nomine Domini,
blessed is he who comes in the name of the Lord.
Your hand that had reached for the door's latch

to free us, froze. No more Q and A.

4 REGRET

After Thomas Wyatt

My schooner filled to brimming with regret
sails in a storm. Breakers flood the deck,
rising slow, in rhythm of deep breaths.
You, radiant as loss, stand at the helm,

clutching the wheel. See, white sails worn brown
with tears of gale-force winds that cracked the engine.
We steer into the eye, all safety gone.
The mind reels with what it can't imagine

of death. Now, limping through rapid currents
between rocks and shale, I dwell on Reason
and Foresight that like trusted tenants
skipped without paying rent, the should-have-done
and might-have-said my torment. Stars blur
tonight as mist consumes the harbor.

5 THE SOUND

A black-white bird you taught me to call skimmer
cruises the point, its red beak straining baywater
for plankton, then arrows past to spin
a U-turn, and wing-flapping, steer

toward the white ashes swelling in the Sound,
an underwater cloud matching a sky-cloud.
At the headland, the water's crosscurrents
oppose each other like your contradictions.

You believed only what could be seen,
though watching shorebirds, you gaze at heaven.
My friend reads of a kestrel hawk's *brute beauty*
and valour and act, oh, air, pride, plume, here . . .
As the white ash-cloud sinks, a figure rises,
fog-like, drenched in morning and in mourning.

"Listen. The tern's whistle. The osprey's call."
                       I hear a chorus, birds anonymous.
"Look there, at the flicker's spotted head."
                       I see white blips in an unspotted blue.

"Look down at the amber rocks and see the rings,
one for the plover, two for the killdeer."
                       I see boulders spangled in sunlight,
                       a settler's dream of gold in a new harbor.

"Now take the binoculars. Look for speckled
ruddy turnstones turning stones for food."
                       Fuzzy. I wipe the lens to focus on
                       marsh grasses, lemon-yellow singed with brown.

So we, who walk wingless, are known by names,
a song, a strut, a night cry, shape of crown,
and like the dowitcher, through zoom lenses,
here and not here. Who are we, you and I?

7 TIME

Pain drags time. Discouraging home callers,
I walked, tracing our sandprints on the shore
and footsteps to the midtown concert hall,

past the park's irises. Broke naan with friends,
and, needing sane talk, said not a word of grief.
Had it been years since the heartbeat stopped?
No, one week. Time doesn't heal grief;
it emphasizes. But it deepens memory.

Diminishing the time he'd been away,
Hamlet rose up at Ophelia's grave.
I loved her more than a thousand brothers.
Dickinson knew *Pain – expands the Time –*
and conversely, *Pain contracts – the Time –*
I cherish pain. Lose it, lose everything.

8 TROMPE L'OEIL

The river that runs East is not a river;
on a clear day you'll see it join the ocean.
Park Avenue is not a park and Lexington
only a battle in the Revolution.

Our post office has moved to a different zone.
Streets are misnamed, and passersby wear masks.
The stars are dimmer for the lights of Starbucks
and for the streetlamps that guide me home—

if there is a home. Nouns fill with helium,
husband, wife, printed on a red balloon
cut loose to fly. I hear your plea,

Never leave my side. I never did.
I never will. But like June's fireflies
you're here and not here. Who are we, you and I?

9 THE VISIT

Compotier, Pitcher and Fruit
Oil on Canvas, by Paul Cézanne

Still life, here meaning still alive. You were
that day, at the Barnes Museum. You sprinted,
caneless, and touched down before a scattering
of apples inert, aglow in greens, gold-reds.

Motion in stasis was the painter's pleasure.
Seemingly immobile, the fruit held power
in check, given an inward pull,
poised to fly off the dish and whirl in air,

then steer to land beside the drained carafe.
Before your body weakened, the electron
microscope your palette, you searched cells

to save lives. Did you know then that life,
empty and full, would come to mean
a hollow pitcher and a plate of apples?

10 FIRST CHILL—THEN STUPOR—
THEN THE LETTING GO—

There is no letting go. Your tenor, singing
Bach off-key, still rises to high ceilings.
Hazel eyes, creased at their corners, dazzle
my bathroom mirror. Your midnight blue

brass-button blazer and your lace-up Oxfords,
for opera nights, are waiting in your closet.
Students and friends have anxious looks. I'm here,
hoisting a wheeler bag, holding a passport

for a strange shore, life incomplete.
One morning a high wave will stall to reveal
its cobalt underside, crash on the rock

I hold, and loosen my grip. In the waves' wash,
a leaking dinghy will sail, motorlesss.
I'll climb aboard and try to bail it out.

Notes

FRANCESCA REDUX
Dante's Inferno, Canto V

MOMENT IN RAPALLO
Phrases in italics are from *A Retrospect*, *How to Read*, and *ABC of Reading*, by Ezra Pound.

Now I recall King Solomon . . . Midrash Tehillim

LIGHT IN GENOA
"In the summer of 1933 Brandeis and Montale began an intense and tormented relationship, the initial phase of which lasted until 1939. It was also the beginning of an intellectual and artistic interaction that would last until the end of their lives." *Eugenio Montale: The Fascist Storm and the Jewish Sunflower*, by David Michael Hertz.

ALIVE AND WELL: TOMB SCULPTURES IN THE
STAGLIENO CEMETERY
These poems and their sculptures are: "Angel" (1882) for Giulio Monteverde (1837–1917); "Widow" for Pienovi (1879) by Giovanni Battista Villa (1832–1899); "Dreamer" for Carlos Erba (1833) by Santo Saccomanno (1833–1914); "Maria Francesca" (who died young, in an auto accident,1909) for Delmas (1909) by Luigi Orengo (1865–1940); "Struggle" for Celle (1893) by Monteverde; "Woman in Sunlight" for Molinari (1920) by Enrico Pacciani Fornari (1886–1958).

Mark Twain, *The Innocents Abroad*. "On every side, as one walks down the middle of the passage, are monuments, tombs, and sculptured figures that are exquisitely wrought and are full of grace and beauty. They are new and snowy; every outline therefore, to us these ranks of bewitching forms are a hundredfold more lovely than the damaged and dingy statuary they have saved from the wreck of ancient art and set up in the galleries of Paris for the worship of the world."

ASCENSION
La Farge's journey to Japan is dramatically rendered by Christopher Benfey in *The Great Wave: Gilded Age Misfits, Chinese Eccentrics, and the Opening of Old Japan.*

STILL LIFES
Paintings are in the Metropolitan Museum, New York City. My gaze fell on "Still Life with Lobster and Fruit," by Abraham van Beyeren, "Still Life with a Glass and Oysters," by Jan Davidsz de Heem," and "Still Life with Fruit, Glassware, and a Wanli Bowl," by Willem Kalf.

GREENWICH VILLAGE STREET TALK
"Frequent capitals are the only marks of verse in Mr. Whitman's writing . . . *Drum-Taps* begins for all the world like verse and turns out to be arrant prose." Henry James in *The Nation*, November 16, 1865.

THE RAINBOW SIGN
The two-line epigraph is from "Mary, Don't You Weep," an African-American spiritual.

BALLADE FOR THE DUKE OF ORLEANS
At Blois, circa 1457, the Duke offered a prize for a ballade containing the line, *Je meurs de soif aupres de la fontaine.* Centuries later, following Richard Wilbur, poets began to take up the challenge.

Acknowledgments

I'm grateful to the editors of the following publications, where poems, sometimes in different forms, were originally published:

Cimarron Review: "Letter from Nicaragua"

The Eloquent Poem: "Ascension," "Eve Speaks"

Fifth Wednesday: "The Wind Game"

The Hudson Review: "Fragments of a Marriage," "Don't Do It," "Geniza," "Light in Genoa," "Because," "Exile"

The Kenyon Review: "The Worst," "The Rooted Bed," "Meteor"

Literary Matters: "Moment in Rapallo," "Moon Plant," "Alive and Well: Tomb Sculptures in the Staglieno Cemetery," "That Summer," "Gone"

Little Star: "Fireplace Bay"

Plume Poetry: "Image Worship," "The Lost Explorers," "El Greco's Vision of St. John," "Rainbow Sign," "Shirt," and "After All"

Southampton Review: "A Love Supreme," "Erratic," "Greenwich Village Street Talk," "The Jetty," "Sleep No More"

Tikkun: "The Sand Dancers"

The Yale Review: "Happiness," "Orchid"

"Gone" was reprinted in *Together in a Sudden Strangeness: American Poets Respond to the Pandemic*.

"Orchid" and "The Rooted Bed" were reprinted by *Poetry Daily*; "El Greco's Vision of St. John" was reprinted in *The Plume Poetry Anthology 3*; "Image Worship" was reprinted in *Still Life with Poem: 100 Natures Mortes in Verse* and in *The Plume Poetry Anthology 4*.

I'm beholden to Baruch College, CUNY, for a fellowship leave endowing this collection, and for continuing faith and support.

My thanks to the Bogliasco Foundation; Yaddo; and the MacDowell Colony for freedom to pursue the work. I'm grateful to friends who have read some of these poems in draft: Alfred Corn, Karl Kirchwey, Carol Muske-Dukes, Elise Paschen, Terese Svoboda, Brian Swann, and my assistant, Jenna Breiter. "Meteor" is for Judy Asnes and Bruce Dow. I thank those who inspired my poems of Italy: Walter Arnold, Massimo Bacigalupo, Ivana Folle, and Alessandra Natale. And my heartfelt gratitude goes to my editor, Ruth Greenstein, for her insight, patience, and fortitude.